The Butterfly Silhouette

2nd Edition

The Butterfly Silhouette

12 Principles for Following Your Soul Where it Must Go

2nd Edition

Jeanne Nangle

Copyright © 2025 by Jeanne Nangle
All rights reserved

The Butterfly Silhouette, 2nd Edition, February 2025

Published by Jeanne Nangle Education, EDH, California

Interior illustrations and cover design by Jared Nangle

Library of Congress Control Number: 2024922878

ISBN 979-8-218-53402-8
Printed in the United States of America

Interior book formatting by Kathryn Marcellino

No part of this publication may be reproduced or transmitted in any form or by any means, electronic or mechanical, including photocopying, recording, scanning, or otherwise, or through any information browsing, storage, or retrieval system.

PUBLISHER'S NOTE
The scanning, uploading, and distribution of this book via the Internet, or any other means is illegal and punishable by law.

This book is not intended to provide and does not constitute medical or other professional advice. The content in The Butterfly Silhouette, 2nd Edition is designed to support, not replace, medical or psychiatric treatment.

This book is dedicated to the people we love who watch over and guide us from the other side of the veil.

Acknowledgments

This book wouldn't be possible without the following people:

To the angels and friends who helped with and supported the original book, you know who you are and I'm eternally grateful for you.

Jared, thank you for illustrating the caterpillar's inner journey and the beautiful book cover design—it's beyond anything I could have envisioned myself. Your patience and willingness to endlessly discuss this book with me have been a great gift.

Jonah, your dedication and courage influence much of this book's heart. Thank you for helping me with the prologue and listening for many years as I've talked about this caterpillar.

I'm deeply grateful to Chelsea, Diane, and Lou for your steady love, support, and presence.

Mark, thank you for telling me to do a second edition and guiding me every step of the way.

And, thank you to my amazing mother, Edda. You deeply bless my life. Thank you for believing in me since day one. Everyone should have such an angel in their life.

Table of Contents

How to Use This Book   i

Caterpillar Poem   iii

Introduction   v

PART I · THE FABLE

Commit to Your Destiny   1

Ask for Guidance   13

Notice What's Beautiful   25

See Yourself on a Soul Level   35

Wish Yourself Compassion   47

Make the Most of Your Time Here   53

Drop into a Hole   63

Let Your Sadness Run Through You   73

Believe in the Plan for You   83

Pry Yourself Free   91

Love Yourself   99

Fill Your Silhouette Out   105

PART II · QUEST NOTES

Principle One	123
Principle Two	129
Principle Three	137
Principle Four	145
Principle Five	155
Principle Six	163
Principle Seven	171
Principle Eight	179
Principle Nine	187
Principle Ten	195
Principle Eleven	203
Principle Twelve	209
Appendix	219

How to Use This Book

The book's first half is a fable in Seussian rhyme that illustrates the *12 Principles of Metamorphosis*. It takes you through personal, emotional, and physical transformation.

The book's second half helps you apply the fable to your life. Each principle is explained with a Toolbox and high-vibration thoughts to help you embody self-belief and self-love. You can work with one principle per week to help you digest the ideas.

My intention is for the book to serve as a complete guide.

Read the book again and again to fulfill your unique destiny.

To your full expression,
~ jeanne

Caterpillar Poem

Jeanne, age 7

Brown and furry
I'm in a hurry
to find a spot
but so far I have not.
And if I don't
I will die
because I have to be,
a butterfly.

Introduction

Six months after my husband had passed away, I woke up in the middle of the night and wrote the beginnings of a book about a caterpillar who doesn't believe she can be a butterfly.

Why did I do that?

What would jolt me from bed in the middle of the night and pull me downstairs?

I never wanted to write a book—it wasn't even a spark of an idea. But the universe had bigger plans for me and placed them inside my sleeping head.

That night, I wrote the first draft. I knew it wasn't anything worth reading yet. So, I did lots of work for many months to improve it and looked for an editor.

After reading and rereading *The Power of Myth* by Joseph Campbell in my 20s, and listening to his interview with Bill Moyers many times, I wanted the heroine to closely follow the *hero's journey*. A writer who had edited books for Joseph Campbell landed on my path, agreed to edit the book, and the first edition was born.

More synchronicities happened after that…

My mother's friend, who we didn't realize was psychic, told me that my husband was a spirit guide of mine and that my book would help many people.

Then, a childhood friend of mine, whom I had lost touch with, remembered the caterpillar poem I'd written in 2nd grade (see above) and recited it to another friend at their high school reunion.

Why would a young child perfectly remember another kid's poem from 2nd grade? Thankfully, the friend she recited the poem to understood the significance.

I saw this as guidance to write a second edition of the book, but I didn't act on it.

A year later, I visited my son in New York. At the time, I felt lost. At this point, I regularly talk to my spirit guides and God. Each day, I meditated in front of his apartment window and asked, *Universe, what would you have me do?*

Then, I trusted. I ate pizza from street vendors, drank Moscow Mules in the local bar, and turned my worries over to the universe.

I didn't receive any guidance while on the trip, but when I got back to California, the guidance to create a second edition of the book was crystal clear.

It started with a guy on LinkedIn, a book promoter I'd never met. He has the same first name as my son and happened to be visiting New York in the same neighborhood, at the same time, as me. He wasn't more significant than that. *You never know where spiritual guidance will come from.*

A lot more happened to help me with this book that I won't go into here.

You might be thinking, *Come on... Does the universe have time or reason to orchestrate so many details about one small book? There are enough books in the world.*

I understand. I've thought the same thing.

But, the *sacred otherness of life* has the time and ability to address infinite details. Remarkable, unexplainable things happen all of the time. If you're closed off to it, you won't see it.

I write this part of the back story to encourage you to keep going with whatever book, idea, project, healing, or inspiration is dropped on your path *that feels like you're meant to do it.*

If you're wondering... *how do I know if I'm meant to do something?*

Excellent question! The answers become clearer as you go through the principles in this book and do the work and play.

We crawl before we fly to our destiny, while something bigger watches over us, helping us along.

> *Inside the beautiful garden,*
> *for those of us who crawl,*
> *metamorphosis is possible,*
> *when we step up to our call.*

Part I - The Fable

PRINCIPLE ONE

Commit to Your Destiny

Commit to Your Destiny

Kat wakes up slowly
on the sunlit garden floor,
stretching her long body,
she waits ten minutes more.

She wonders what the day will bring,
the minutes and full hours,
of climbing trees and eating leaves
and petals from moist flowers.

THE BUTTERFLY SILHOUETTE

Jolting quickly from her thoughts,
it's time to start the day.
Kat sees a cluster of spiders
and promptly makes her way.

COMMIT TO YOUR DESTINY

The tallest spider turns to her
on long and lovely legs.
Kat is quickly conscious of
her limbs as short as pegs.

"Caterpillar, are you in the race today?"
the spider routinely asks.
Kat says, "No, not me, not today.
I've a million other tasks."

THE BUTTERFLY SILHOUETTE

She's working on a project
of combining leaves and petals,
to protect her soft long body
from the pricking, stinging nettles.

Kat loves simple days of
meandering on the ground,
doing this and that
and not running round and round.

COMMIT TO YOUR DESTINY

"Sorry, we will miss you,"
the spider sincerely states.
Leggy bugs are so polite,
which Kat appreciates.

THE BUTTERFLY SILHOUETTE

Kat spies her enemy, a beastly bug,
although she'd rather not.
Her dotted eyes avoid him,
but he sees her on the spot.

"Look who's here!" the bug yells,
bouncing like a bee.
"If you want to climb this tree,
you'll have to get past me!"

COMMIT TO YOUR DESTINY

Kat stops quickly in her tracks
to avoid the boring beast,
while he is busy boasting
to five other bugs, at least.

She inches right behind him
and leaps onto the trunk,
then trips over some tacky sap
and stumbles with a clunk!

THE BUTTERFLY SILHOUETTE

Somersaulting to the ground
as bugs watch from nearby,
I know there's something more in me,
Kat whispers with a sigh.

COMMIT TO YOUR DESTINY

Nearby bugs dart in and out,
each gawking as they dangle.
"Sixteen legs are a lot to handle
and way too easily tangled."

Kat calmly collects herself
and her tangled thoughts,
and crawls to a safer place
beneath the sun's great watts.

PRINCIPLE TWO

Ask for Guidance

Ask for Guidance

That night Kat tosses and turns a lot,
still troubled by her day.
The leaves beneath her body
won't lay the perfect way.

She looks into the starry sky,
wondering what she'll see,
"If anyone is out there,
will you please come talk to me?"

THE BUTTERFLY SILHOUETTE

The wind swirls around her.
The trees begin to sway.
Something strange is happening
tempting Kat to crawl away.

ASK FOR GUIDANCE

A gorgeous butterfly appears,
dropping from the night,
landing her body carefully
beneath the bright moonlight.

"Goodness, what a frazzled flight."
the butterfly kindly says.
"I've been flying for so long
I'm woozy in the head!
Tell me what is troubling you?"
the butterfly softly queries.
"The garden is always listening,"
she says a wee bit wearied.

THE BUTTERFLY SILHOUETTE

"Is there more within me?"
Kat bends her neck to see.
"I feel something within me
I must do or be."

ASK FOR GUIDANCE

The butterfly takes in a breath
and slowly blows it out.
She understands Kat's question
and knows what it's about.

THE BUTTERFLY SILHOUETTE

"Your question is a good one
and deserves some tender thought.
Let's pack it in your suitcase
and leave here on the spot.
I'm taking you to a special place,"
the butterfly declares.
"There's so much for you to see.
Are your sixteen legs prepared?"

ASK FOR GUIDANCE

"Hello!" is barked in front of them,
as the beastly bug jumps in.
Kat flops and flinches,
nearly shedding off her skin.

"Aren't you two a sorry pair!"
the bug observes out loud.
"Tell me what you're doing here!"
he bosses beneath a cloud.

THE BUTTERFLY SILHOUETTE

"None of this is your concern!"
the butterfly says quite peeved.
"Annoying bugs infuriate me,
now flap your wings and leave!"

The beastly bug is much too small
to tangle with this pair.
So he leaps into the sky
and flies into blue air.

ASK FOR GUIDANCE

Kat and the butterfly
begin their journey together,
intent to keep on moving,
through beastly bugs and weather.

PRINCIPLE THREE

Notice What's Beautiful

Notice What's Beautiful

"I rarely leave the garden,
especially so late,"
Kat informs the butterfly
as she crawls outside the gate.

"Yes, pay close attention,"
the butterfly kindly says.
"We have a ways to go,
it's best to look ahead."

THE BUTTERFLY SILHOUETTE

While up along the sandy path
their eyes see in the distance,
a blanket of green grasses,
laid out for their assistance.
The grasses are finely dimpled
with copious colors of spring,
like brilliant whites and yellows,
and violets about to sing.

NOTICE WHAT'S BEAUTIFUL

"This is beautiful!"
says Kat amply astounded.
"What's this place you've brought me to?
What corner have we rounded?"

THE BUTTERFLY SILHOUETTE

A young, precocious butterfly
comes in quickly from the rear.
"You're in a special place
we all visit every year.
Here's a newsy riddle
you'll most likely want to hear.
Listen very closely
with your caterpillar ear:

What has colorful wings
and stays off the ground?
Please take a guess
while you rest on the mound."

NOTICE WHAT'S BEAUTIFUL

"Won't you please tell
me what this is about?"
Kat is confused and
her legs are worn out.

THE BUTTERFLY SILHOUETTE

"The answer is:
A butterfly like me!
One day you'll be the flying bug
you're designed to be!"

Then, the erudite butterfly
takes off in flight.
She riddles her riddle
and flies from their sight.

NOTICE WHAT'S BEAUTIFUL

Kat says, "I'm meant to be a butterfly,
 with wings, antennas, and such?
  It doesn't seem too likely
  that I will change that much."

PRINCIPLE FOUR

See Yourself on a Soul Level

See Yourself on a Soul Level

"Caterpillar, pack up your doubt,
you've someone to meet.
We'll arrive at her cave
in fifty-four feet.
She's a great Monarch butterfly,
both wise and mysterious.
She helps bugs like you
because doubt is so serious."

THE BUTTERFLY SILHOUETTE

They arrive at the cave,
wide-eyed and excited,
as Kat's faithful fear
is promptly ignited.

SEE YOURSELF ON A SOUL LEVEL

"Hello, my new visitors!
I heard you were coming.
Please excuse all the noise from
that hummingbird humming."

THE BUTTERFLY SILHOUETTE

As Kat cautiously enters
the Monarch's dark cave,
she looks to her friend,
a half smile she gave.

The air drops onto them,
heavy and thick,
coating their bodies
like wax on a wick.

Kat inhales the smell
of water and rocks,
as time disappears
in this world of no clocks.

SEE YOURSELF ON A SOUL LEVEL

In front of her is a pond,
floating quietly in the middle.
Kat wonders about its purpose,
is this another riddle?

THE BUTTERFLY SILHOUETTE

"I see you admiring
my magical pond.
I assure you it's something
of which you'll be fond.
When you look in the water,"
the monarch explains,
"you'll see your destiny,
you'll know it by name."

SEE YOURSELF ON A SOUL LEVEL

Kat stares into
the water beyond.
She sees *her reflection*
inside the still pond.

THE BUTTERFLY SILHOUETTE

Suddenly, wings shoot from the body
as soft as silk crepe.
Kat's reflection morphs into
a magnificent shape!

The wings turn to orange,
deep yellows, and blues.
The colors spray like rainbows
in brilliant bold hues.

SEE YOURSELF ON A SOUL LEVEL

Stunned, Kat watches
in dumbfounded surprise,
watching it float
in front of her eyes.

The fluttering reflection
has something to say.
Its words float through the water
and come out this way:

"Deep down inside,
you know who you are.
You need to look closer
and don't stray too far."

THE BUTTERFLY SILHOUETTE

Then, the butterfly reflection
slowly starts sinking.
Its beautiful wings
are now shriveling and shrinking.

While waving from the water
it continues to fall,
until nothing is left of it,
nothing at all.

PRINCIPLE FIVE

Wish Yourself Compassion

Wish Yourself Compassion

Kat stares blankly
into the pond,
befuddled and troubled—
the reflection is gone!

THE BUTTERFLY SILHOUETTE

She starts to wobble
and becomes very dizzy.
The fuzz on her back
from the moisture is frizzy.

Kat collapses
into a small mound.
The cave is so quiet
you can't hear a sound.

The butterfly gathers her
with widening wings,
and carries her out
to some nearby cool springs.

WISH YOURSELF COMPASSION

In the fresh air,
Kat finally wakes.
She turns to her friend,
although her voice shakes.

"Why is it so hard—
this change for myself?
Is it my fear?
Is there anything else?"

The butterfly says,
since she is so wise,
what she's said to others
before they took to the skies…

THE BUTTERFLY SILHOUETTE

"Wish yourself compassion
for all that you are.
Your dark and your light
come from the same star.
The compassion you feel
beginning with yourself
will spread across the garden
to everyone else."

PRINCIPLE SIX

Make the Most of Your Time Here

Make the Most of Your Time Here

They continue on their journey,
chomping and chewing flowers,
hoping to find a place to sleep
for several restful hours.

The butterfly smells the scent of spring,
as winter has long passed.
Mosquitoes are buzzing about the marsh—
things change so awfully fast.

THE BUTTERFLY SILHOUETTE

While pondering the moment
and moving with her thoughts,
the butterfly notices her thorax
is tender in some spots.

There's a single strange sensation,
she hasn't had before.
Am I feeling queasy
or something much, much more?

Stopping for a quick moment
to take a long, deep breath,
her inner clock is ticking,
the time has come for death.

MAKE THE MOST OF YOUR TIME HERE

The butterfly accepts this,
as butterflies often do,
but she isn't nearly ready
to leave the caterpillar too.

THE BUTTERFLY SILHOUETTE

"Is something wrong?"
Kat worriedly asks.
"You're so quiet
and not moving very fast."

MAKE THE MOST OF YOUR TIME HERE

The butterfly says, "We don't get to stay
on this earth forever.
Our time is quite short
regardless of our endeavor.
The truth is—
it's time for my body to die.
We may not feel ready,
but we need to say goodbye."

THE BUTTERFLY SILHOUETTE

Kat is stunned,
her eyes begin tearing.
She does not believe
a thing she is hearing.

"What are you saying?
There must be a mistake!
You can't leave me now,
or my heart will surely break."

The butterfly thinks,
I love the caterpillar too,
but I need to tell her,
there's more she has to do.

MAKE THE MOST OF YOUR TIME HERE

"You're meant to be a butterfly,
despite your inner strife.
I say this because I care so much,
you must change your life."

Then, the butterfly is gone
as fast as she came.
The caterpillar's heart
would not be the same.

THE BUTTERFLY SILHOUETTE

PRINCIPLE SEVEN

Drop into a Hole

Drop into a Hole

Kat lays limply
spread out in the dirt,
her legs droop to one side,
her long body one hurt.

Rolling onto her legs
she falls into a hole,
filled with mole carcass
and grub, the mole stole.

THE BUTTERFLY SILHOUETTE

Now she is deep
in this dark, eerie place.
She doesn't even care,
she just buries her face.

*Just leave me in here
and kick in the dirt.
At least in this hole,
I can fill in the hurt.*

DROP INTO A HOLE

An industrious ladybug
flies by the hole,
looks into its depths and yells,
"Come out you fool!
Staying in that hole,
won't help a thing.
Come be in the garden
where birds like to sing."

THE BUTTERFLY SILHOUETTE

"I DETEST singing birds
and your all-knowing smile."
Kat says, "Just go away,
I'll be in here awhile."

DROP INTO A HOLE

Many days pass and
Kat needs some food.
She crawls out of the hole
when the grub is all chewed.

Kat shakes off her body,
moves two of her feet,
the rest seem to follow,
they perform like a fleet.

She keeps moving forward,
one leg then the other,
proceeding in unison
to feebly recover.

THE BUTTERFLY SILHOUETTE

Out of nowhere, the beastly bug
blazes right onto Kat's path,
poking her anger,
inciting her wrath.

Kat says, "Stop buzzing around me,
must you persist?
Why in the garden
do you even exist?"

DROP INTO A HOLE

"Caterpillars on quests
think you're better than us.
Why don't you quit?
Quests aren't worth the fuss."

THE BUTTERFLY SILHOUETTE

Kat leaves the hole
and continues on her way,
not knowing what to do
on this abysmal day.

PRINCIPLE EIGHT

Let Your Sadness Run Through You

Let Your Sadness Run Through You

Kat sees a large puddle
to soak all her pain.
It's a *well of all healing*
created by the rain.

THE BUTTERFLY SILHOUETTE

To her tiny eyes
the puddle looks like a lake,
dark and foreboding,
its contents opaque.

Long willowy shadows
hover above
this mysterious puddle
Kat's skeptical of.

LET YOUR SADNESS RUN THROUGH YOU

Kat wonders, *Should I crawl away?*
Is being here a mistake?
Her sixteen legs stall
as she approaches the murky lake.

THE BUTTERFLY SILHOUETTE

"Come inside caterpillar,"
a husky voice plays.
"Step into the puddle's depths,
you don't need to be afraid."

Kat asks, "Isn't this just a puddle
pooling underneath a tree?"
Kat doesn't see
there's more a puddle can be.

LET YOUR SADNESS RUN THROUGH YOU

The voice says, "Your intellect won't work in here,
it's useless at these depths.
Leave your logic on the shore,
over by those stoney steps.

This is a well of all healing—
what doesn't heal will continue to bleed.
Let your sadness run right through you,
though it's very hard indeed."

THE BUTTERFLY SILHOUETTE

Kat barely listens,
it's what she has to do,
but she doesn't have the stamina
to feel more sadness too.

"I'm on a quest to nowhere.
I've no idea in the least.
Now, my dearest friend has died.
I can barely crawl to the east."

LET YOUR SADNESS RUN THROUGH YOU

The husky voice asserts itself
as Kat begins to crumble.
Its wisdom comes from many years
guiding creatures through their stumbles.

The voice says, "By entering *the well*,
a place we all must go,
you'll discover the deepest mysteries,
but one needs to go below."

Kat is powerfully pulled
from the safety of the shore,
letting go of its soft edges,
she's more frightened than before.

PRINCIPLE NINE

Believe in the Plan for You

Believe in the Plan for You

Shaking in the water,
not knowing what to do,
Kat plunges beneath the surface
of the puddle's purplish hue.

Underneath the water,
Kat can't believe her eyes.
It's her loving, beautiful butterfly,
sixteen times her normal size!

THE BUTTERFLY SILHOUETTE

"Where've you been?" asks Kat.
"I've missed you very much!
I'm surprised to see you down here,
so close I can almost touch!"

BELIEVE IN THE PLAN FOR YOU

The butterfly says, "I had important things
it was time for me to do.
I came back down here briefly
just to talk to you.
I want you to know I'm fine.
I'm where I need to be.
I'm watching everything you do,
there's nothing I won't see."

THE BUTTERFLY SILHOUETTE

"So, you're going back?
You're not here for good?"
Kat's heart breaks again.
She misunderstood.

BELIEVE IN THE PLAN FOR YOU

"I'm sorry I had to leave you."
the butterfly softly says.
"Recall your *reflection in the cave*,
focus there instead.
Let me tell you a secret
that few in the garden know—
You have someone you're meant to be,
though you don't think it's so."

THE BUTTERFLY SILHOUETTE

The butterfly says goodbye,
like she did before,
taking her soul out for a ride
through the garden's swinging door.

PRINCIPLE TEN

Pry Yourself Free

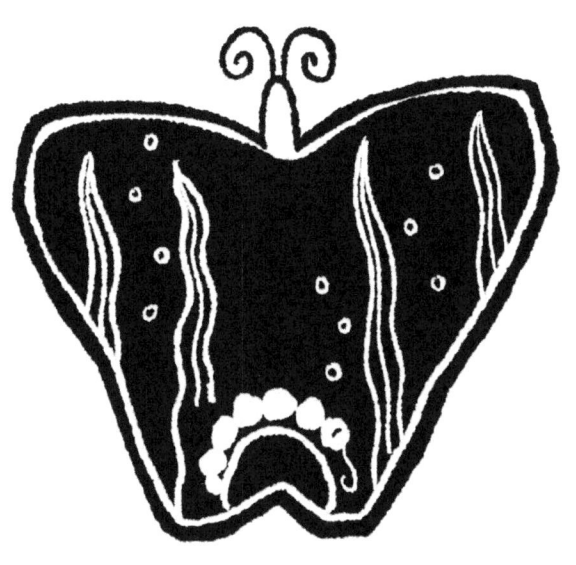

Pry Yourself Free

Kat drops quickly,
deep into the puddle,
kicking all sixteen legs
to help her mind un-muddle.

As she swims deeper,
her beating heart tightens,
it contracts and hardens
as she grows more frightened.

Until Kat can handle
the terrible tension no more,
her tears bubble outward
and desperately pour.

THE BUTTERFLY SILHOUETTE

Kat cries in the puddle,
she cannot sleep.
Three days and three nights,
all she does is weep.

The puddle grows larger
filling up with Kat's tears,
as she spits drops of salt
she has tasted for years.

PRY YOURSELF FREE

Kat swims deeper
away from the light,
down inside the puddle
where the color is night.

She finally hits
the puddle's hard floor,
when her legs are pinched under
one large stone or more.

THE BUTTERFLY SILHOUETTE

Now Kat is stuck
in one exact spot,
trying her hardest to move,
and yet move, she cannot.

She twists and contorts
to pry herself free
from the stoney impingement
she cannot quite see.

"Please let me go,"
Kat prays to the stone.
"I don't want to be stuck here.
I want to go home."

PRY YOURSELF FREE

Kat keeps digging
until she is sore,
using all of her strength,
to move her legs more.

The stone is immovable
as it settles with a thud,
slippery and buried
and cradled in mud.

THE BUTTERFLY SILHOUETTE

She lies on the stone
and continues to cry,
overcome by the fear
that she'll possibly die.

"I love you,"
Kat hears herself say.
She leans into the stone
and the stone moves its way.

PRINCIPLE ELEVEN
Love Yourself

Love Yourself

Kat begins floating.
What is this feeling?
Have I died too…
and from death, I am reeling?

But Kat isn't dead,
not nearly, not yet.
She's rising to the surface
of the puddle all wet.

THE BUTTERFLY SILHOUETTE

Kat crosses a threshold
as some creatures do.
In the puddle's dark depths,
she learns what is true.

LOVE YOURSELF

"Hello, caterpillar,"
It's the beastly bug's face!
Somehow he's here
in this faraway place.

But, the bug doesn't matter
to Kat anymore.
He's distant from view
as she paddles to shore.

THE BUTTERFLY SILHOUETTE

Kat emerges from the
puddle with new eyes,
into the garden
underneath spotty skies.

She looks to the sky
with eyes that can see,
*"Keep healing my heart,
so I can be free."*

PRINCIPLE TWELVE

Fill Your Silhouette Out

Fill Your Silhouette Out

Still wet from the puddle,
Kat looks over the garden,
its colors and shapes
and the way dead worms harden.

Kat notices a strange form
in the garden ahead.
It's curvy and black.
It has wings and a head.

Moving a bit closer,
Kat gets a good look.
It's plain to her eyes,
her whole body shook.

THE BUTTERFLY SILHOUETTE

It's a grand silhouette,
a beautiful butterfly,
floating in space
against the blue sky.

FILL YOUR SILHOUETTE OUT

Its wings are immense,
a canvas of black,
but vacant inside
from the front to the back.

Kat understands
what this is about.
But she isn't quite ready
to fill her silhouette out.

THE BUTTERFLY SILHOUETTE

"Why do you pause?
What do you believe that you lack?"
A voice says watching her
hold herself back.

FILL YOUR SILHOUETTE OUT

Kat asks, "Is it too big,
this new life I see?
The largeness of the wings
terrifies me."

A momentary fear
put a chill in the air
as it quickly subsides
and is no longer there.

THE BUTTERFLY SILHOUETTE

The voice asserts, "The butterfly silhouette
will not be denied.
This life is meant for you.
It's time to step inside."

FILL YOUR SILHOUETTE OUT

Slowly, Kat crawls up
to her silhouette,
places each foot inside,
then plunges in all wet.

As the final leg crosses
the tiny threshold,
Kat's new life takes shape
and begins to unfold.

THE BUTTERFLY SILHOUETTE

Unaware that she knows this,
Kat forms leaves in a pile
and creates a chrysalis
that she sleeps for a while.

Kat stays there for days
while her whole body changes,
every part of her being
completely rearranges.

FILL YOUR SILHOUETTE OUT

When Kat awakes,
she notices her wings.
Her eyes fill with tears
from all that change brings.

She unfolded her wings
in a moment of bliss.
"I had no idea
it would be like this."

THE BUTTERFLY SILHOUETTE

Practicing for days
Kat gets used to her wings,
bobbing amongst flowers,
unafraid of bee stings.

One hot afternoon
while up in the air,
she hears someone calling,
"Can anyone hear me out there?"

FILL YOUR SILHOUETTE OUT

Looking to the ground,
for who placed the call,
Kat sees a caterpillar climbing
trying hard not to fall.

Kat swoops swiftly
down to the ground.
She's getting very good
at fluttering around!

THE BUTTERFLY SILHOUETTE

Kat says, "Hello brave caterpillar,
how do you do?
I heard you calling,
what's troubling you?"

FILL YOUR SILHOUETTE OUT

"Garden life is hard for me,"
the young caterpillar stresses.
"I hardly feel brave at all,"
she earnestly confesses.

Kat helps the caterpillar
crawl outside her gate.
"Come with me, there's much to see.
Let's go, it's getting late."

THE BUTTERFLY SILHOUETTE

With that, they form a friendship
and embark on a new quest.
They visit puddles along the way,
and well, you know all the rest.

Part II - Quest Notes

1. Commit to Your Destiny

For a moment, think of yourself as this caterpillar in the garden *climbing trees and eating leaves and petals from moist flowers.*

You like climbing trees and eating leaves, but you feel there's something more to you. *You are compelled toward something you must do or be.*

Possibly, you want to heal your heart, express something meaningful, create something you love, make a difference, connect with something bigger than you, etc. I had a deep desire for all of this.

This causes great confusion—it's not just one thing the soul must do. It's a mixture of things.

As you progress through the *12 Principles of Metamorphosis,* you'll recognize the silhouette of *who you're meant to be* floating in the distance.

It's where your soul must go.

In general, your destiny is to…

Make the world better in your specific way.

Learn soul lessons and heal your heart.

Find the best soul connections and people to do your work with.

Live with joy and bliss because you're being who you're meant to be.

Commit to your destiny. You have a specific reason for being born.

If you're anything like my caterpillar, you doubt that the universe is interested in your one small voice. But, it is.

So, whether your one small voice is heard softly or loudly, commit to using it somehow, someplace.

Toolbox

1. As you uncover your destiny, commit to it.

2. Start and end each day in gratitude. Look for what you're grateful for. When you're grateful, you're not afraid.

3. **Read the high-vibe thoughts for each principle.**

Read as many of the thoughts listed for each principle as you want each day. Don't overwhelm yourself. *Think of good thoughts as eating something healthy and nutritious!*

This tool we call *thoughts*—is powerful.

As you read high-vibe thoughts, notice your energy rising. Even if it's temporary, this will show you the energetic power within thoughts.

COMMIT TO YOUR DESTINY

High-Vibe Thinking™

I am committed to expressing what is within me.
I am allowing my highest truth and greatest healing.
I respect what I need.
I am allowing what I need to come to the surface.
I will not let fear stand in my way.
I am moving forward, one leg then the other.
My path is my own and only I can walk it.
I am walking my unique path.
I am here for a reason. I am committed to expressing that reason.
I will not let others' limited thinking determine my thinking.
I will not limit myself and what I can accomplish.
I am healing my past so I don't bring it into the present.
Whenever I feel less than or not enough in any way, I allow it and breathe.
I am enough for what my soul is here to do.
I will NOT stand in the way of my soul.
I am strong enough to pursue what scares me.
I am strong enough to express how I feel.
I am letting go of needing approval from others.
I am much bigger than my limiting thoughts and the limiting thoughts of others.
I am determined to be all I can be.

I am excited to fulfill my potential in this life.
I am grateful for BLANK.
I am grateful for my life.
I am grateful for this body.
I am grateful for a place to live.
I am grateful for my talents.
I am grateful that I get to do this.

Book Group Prompts

1. What does the beastly bug represent for you? ie: *fear of Blank, self-doubt, not-enoughness…*
2. Do you believe you have a destiny?
3. If so, what is one of the things you're meant to do with your life?
4. In what ways are you moving towards your destiny?

2. Ask for Guidance

A magnificent universe is guiding you on your quest to *who you're designed to be*.

This is the hardest thing to believe when you're crawling.

Yet, crawling helps you uncover important information about yourself.

The confusion, failures, and heartache give you the friction you need so you'll dig deeper.

THE BUTTERFLY SILHOUETTE

Ask the universe to help and hold you each step of the way.

As you do, you'll feel a greater and greater supportive Presence in some form.

Forms of Support

The Sacred Otherness of Life
A higher power is looking over and helping you. *What this is for you is a very personal decision.*

About six major world religions, 10,000 smaller religions, and many spiritual and non-spiritual belief systems attempt to guide us in human life. *Choose the belief system that feels **true for you**—not true for your parents, partner, friends, or people with loud voices.* Be true to yourself.

Soul Connections
These people can be your partner, spouse, family, friends, or even strangers who profoundly impact you. It feels like you've known them before. *These people will reflect to you what your soul is here for, to help you see yourself in a true light.*

For example, my husband told me way before I was doing this work, "*You're all about service.*" I had never seen that quality in myself before he said that. I was meant to hear that from him. He was meant to tell me that.

Spirit Guides and Guardian Angels
Beings of light are assigned to comfort and support you on your path to your highest good and greatest healing.

Books, mentors, and leaders
These will inform you and lead you along your path.

Recognizing Guidance

Recognizing when the *sacred otherness of life* is helping you along your soul's path is more art than science.

However, when your immediate thought is: *That's a coincidence*, it's usually not. "Coincidence is God's way of remaining anonymous."

Keep this in mind when you're quick to discount an event as a coincidence, an accident, or meaningless. Your intuition about your life increases as you do this soul work and play.

ASK FOR GUIDANCE

Toolbox

1. Ask for guidance and support when lost, confused, afraid, or struggling.

Drop into your heart and say: *Please help me with BLANK. I am afraid of BLANK, please give me clarity and guidance.*

Receive guidance by saying *Thank you.* For example, when you feel comfort, nudged in a certain direction, courage, or insight… say: *Thank you.*

This tells the universe that you're paying attention to what's happening in your life and receiving the help that's given to you.

2. Ask yourself: *Do my beliefs empower me? Do I feel loved and cared for by this universe?*

Do my beliefs diminish me or others in ANY way? This is a universe where we're all learning lessons.

3. Make time to be quiet each day where you're not doing anything: no screens, no talking, no thinking, no asking—just watch your breath and let your thoughts come and go.

4. Keep a journal of the times you've received spiritual guidance. Draw it. Write it—have fun with it. When you see how often it's happening, you'll notice it more often.

High-Vibe Thinking™

I am listening.
I am not alone in this.
I am open to the intelligence around me.
I am resourceful.
I feel your Presence. I feel your Presence. I feel your Presence.
I can get the help I need.
I can get the answers I need.
I realize this is an abundant universe.
I am receiving abundance.
I don't have all the answers and that's OK.
I listen to advice when I ask for it.
I am open to the wisdom around me.
I am open and willing while focusing on what I'm creating.
I love learning new things about my life.
I love learning new things about myself.
As I learn, I grow.
When I let go, answers flow to me.
I am open to guidance about what will serve the highest good.
I am open to guidance about what will help me heal.
I am listening.

Book Group Prompts

1. Do you ask for spiritual guidance about the challenges in your life?
2. How often do you turn to guidance and support?
3. Do you feel heard? Elaborate on how you know you're being heard… or not being heard.

3. Notice What's Beautiful

Notice what's beautiful. Notice what's positive. Notice what's working in your life.

This doesn't mean ignoring your problems and feelings. Just give plenty of attention and energy to what's beautiful.

Don't skew to the negative—which we tend to do when upset, hurting, neglected, or afraid.

There are many kinds of negative thoughts, but the ones that especially hurt the soul are thoughts that diminish you or your potential.

THE BUTTERFLY SILHOUETTE

For example, in Principle Two of the fable, Kat says to the butterfly:

> "Is there more within me?"
> Kat bends her neck to see.
> "I feel something within me
> I must do and be."

She has this deep sense of herself, which is beautiful. Yet, later in Principle Three, she says…

> "I'm meant to be a butterfly,
> with wings, antennas, and such?
> It doesn't seem too likely
> that I can change that much."

It doesn't seem too likely that I can change that much.

Her deep sense of herself turns to doubt. This is what we do. We feel there's more to us—and then we doubt it.

Self-doubt needs to be healed—and it takes time.

NOTICE WHAT'S BEAUTIFUL

For now, notice when you're thinking: *It's too much. I'm not good enough. It's taking too long. Others are doing it better. I don't have what it takes. I can't do it. I don't know what I'm doing. It's not in the cards for me.*

When your thoughts go in that direction, gently catch yourself and breathe. Simply notice and tell yourself: *No, I'm not doing that.* This is the beginning of separating yourself from your thoughts.

What you focus on gets bigger. For example, if you focus on your weaknesses, you'll feel you're not good enough. If you focus on how you've been hurt, you'll feel more hurt. If you think about what you fear, you'll be more afraid.

As you improve the quality of your thinking and heal your heart, you're being true to your soul.

Toolbox

1. Notice your negative thinking. Catch thoughts that limit you, discourage you, and tell you you're not enough.

When you notice, pause and breathe. Now breathe again. **Increased awareness begins the process of transforming your negative thinking into high-vibration thinking**. This takes time and effort, but you can do it. If you're reading this book, you're already on your way.

2. Notice your energy throughout the day… *by noticing your feelings*. In your journal, write down your emotions. Notice which emotions come up most often.

High-vibration emotions include peace, joy, love, acceptance, willingness, neutrality, courage, warmth, aliveness, openness, excitement, and relaxation.

Examples of low-vibration emotions are shame, guilt, apathy, or fear. These feelings are part of being human and *nothing is wrong with them*. However, they're uncomfortable and/or painful.

NOTICE WHAT'S BEAUTIFUL

For now, simply notice your emotions *without judgment.* Most of us bounce from one emotion to another on both ends of the spectrum. You will work with this more in Principles 7 through 10.

3. Write down what is working in your life in your journal: What is positive right now? What brings you joy? What makes you feel valued?

4. Take time to *not think*. Sit quietly, focus on your breath, and quiet your mind for a few minutes a day or more. Again, this takes practice and it's doing more for you than you think!

High-Vibe Thinking™

I notice the quality of my thinking.
I focus my attention on what's beautiful.
I focus my attention on what's working well in my life.
I allow healing and growth.
I allow my feelings.
I accept my feelings.
All of my feelings are valid.
I am creating from my soul.
I love creating this.
I am creating a plan to increase the enjoyment of my life.
I choose to trust instead of doubt.
I choose to trust instead of fear.
I can do this.
I am doing this.
I know good things are on the way.
I am healthy and strong.
I am on the right path.
I feel loved and cared for.
I am willing to adapt.
I am flexible.
I enjoy my life.
I attract great people into my life.

NOTICE WHAT'S BEAUTIFUL

I am grateful for what I have.
I'm right where I need to be.
My life is precious to me.
I enjoy this.
I am honest with myself.
I am relaxed and calm.
I allow what is great in me to come forward.
I have enough energy and talent to do this.
I am grateful to my body for carrying me.
I am grateful to my mind for empowering me.
I attract the right opportunities.
I cancel negative thoughts and stories.
I noticed that BLANK was kind to me.
I noticed that the conversation went better than expected.
I noticed how calm I felt.
I notice how much energy I feel.
I notice how nice the sun feels.
I notice how blue the sky is.
I notice how my body feels better.

Book Group Prompts

1. What is working well in your life?
2. When you notice you're thinking negatively, what do you do now?
3. With negative thinking, what will you do going forward?

4. See Yourself on a Soul Level

Look at your soul's potential.

> "Deep down inside
> you know who you are.
> *You need to look closer*
> and don't stray too far."

There is a plan for your life. *It's an outline of what is possible based on your choices.*

THE BUTTERFLY SILHOUETTE

In the magical cave, when Kat looks into the pond and sees her reflection, she sees *what's possible* for her.

> Suddenly, wings shoot from the body
> as soft as silk crepe.
> Kat's reflection morphs into
> a magnificent shape!
>
> The wings turn to orange,
> deep yellows, and blues.
> The colors spray like rainbows
> in brilliant bold hues.

Kat sees her destiny inside the pond. While she doesn't believe it yet, she sees it.

Seeing it is the beginning of the transformation.

Uncover what your soul is here to give and learn. The Toolbox below will help you look closer—and *don't stray too far*.

Toolbox

In your quest for self-knowledge and fulfilling your potential these questions and prompts will help you. It's OK to not have the answers right away. Self-discovery is a process.

1. What do I feel I *must do?*

Help others, heal others, lead others, teach others, express something, be a good example, or change something...

2. What are my gifts, my treasures?

I do this very well. I notice that I'm often recognized for being good at… As I'm doing it I feel self-worth and self-value.

3. What comes naturally to me?

I've always done this, especially as a child.

4. What do I love?

As I'm doing it, I'm filled with love.

5. What do I enjoy?

As I'm doing it, I'm filled with joy.

6. What makes me feel alive?

When I'm doing it I lose track of time. I feel lost in it.

7. What have I had *prior knowledge* about? (If anything)

Prior knowledge is when you haven't learned about or been exposed to a subject; yet, you're deeply drawn to it. You understand it at an intuitive level.

Find a way to bring more of the things you're drawn to into your life.

Even if you're not paid, if it's not your job or career, find a way to fit your gifts and talents into your life… *because it's given to you, within the soul, as a gift to be used and shared.*

Some ideas are, I must:

Write a book
Lead people
Heal people
Create things

SEE YOURSELF ON A SOUL LEVEL

Make things
Express this
Build this
Heal this
Write this specific book
Play the piano
Learn martial arts
Learn a new skill
Run my own business
Go back to college
Get an advanced degree
Make people laugh
Write poetry
Ease people's suffering
Broaden people's perspectives
Learn how to do something very specific
Have children
Be married
Be a BLANK

8. Create a preliminary plan for what you will do NEXT to use *one of your gifts*. Don't be intense or heavy about the plan. Have the plan come from joy.

Write down 3 things you'll need to do to carry out the plan.

Read this plan each day.

When you begin getting nervous and afraid of failure, pause, breathe, and move forward. Remind yourself, *this is meant to fill you up*. Life can be joyful and fun—even though there's learning along the way.

Choose thoughts that support you being happy in your life and expressing yourself fully.

SEE YOURSELF ON A SOUL LEVEL

High-Vibe Thinking™

I have a reason for being here.
My soul is here for a reason.
I am committed to fulfilling that reason.
I feel safe enough to look closer.
I believe in myself.
I am excited to do all that I'm capable of.
May I be strong. OR, I am strong.
May I be brave. OR, I am brave.
May I overcome my fear of failure and rejection. OR, I am overcoming my fear.
I can do this.
I can handle this.
I am more than my limiting thoughts.
I see the vision for my life.
I am making time for my envisioned outcome.
I receive any insight I need.
As I heal my life, I create it.
As I heal my life, I grow in self-love.
As I let go of the expectations of others, I am free.
I depend solely on myself and God/Source/Universe for my happiness, security, and inner peace.
I will not let my fear and doubt stop me.
I enjoy self-knowledge.

THE BUTTERFLY SILHOUETTE

I am good at _____

I am talented at _____

I love _____ about myself.

I am passionate about _____

I have prior knowledge about _____
_____

I feel *most alive* when _____
_____

I feel I *must* _____

I embrace all that I am.

I accept all that I am.

I am growing self-love.

I express what is within my soul.

I pay attention to the clues to my destiny.

I intend to heal _____

Book Group Prompts

1. Do you make time for self-reflection?
2. Do you reflect on why your soul is here?
3. With one gift or talent you have, are you using it and how are you using it?

5. Wish Yourself Compassion

Have deep compassion for the pain and challenges you've experienced. Instead of criticizing yourself, choose kindness and gentle honesty.

Listening to your inner critic makes it easy to see your flaws. *This habit of self-criticism needs healing.*

We judge ourselves far too often. This judgment comes from the ego and leads to unnecessary suffering. When you criticize and blame yourself, it only deepens feelings of shame, hopelessness, and inadequacy.

THE BUTTERFLY SILHOUETTE

Instead of self-judgment, choose kindness and self-honesty. *Self-honesty, when paired with compassion, nurtures self-love.* It lets you face challenges while giving yourself the patience to work through them.

Compassion creates space for growth and positive change.

Affirm: *I am putting down this heavy weight of self-criticism. I have compassion for myself. I am healing my life.*

Toolbox

1. Sometimes, you need a quick way to re-center and bring compassion into your day. A mindful self-compassion break is a short practice you can do anytime you're feeling stressed. Try this when you're judging yourself…

Pause and breathe: Stop what you're doing and take a few gentle deep breaths.

Speak kind words: Use a comforting thought like, *May I be at ease,* or simply *I am enough.*

2. Journaling with self-compassion develops an ongoing practice of kindness toward yourself. Writing with self-compassion is a great way to embody self-love.

How to journal with self-compassion:

Write about challenges: Reflect on a difficult situation you faced recently. Write how *you feel* about it. For example… *I feel Blank.*

Practice self-compassion: Respond to yourself with kindness and compassion. For example, *it must have been so hard to go through that. Or, it was really hard to go through that. I feel for myself.* See the list of high-vibe thoughts below.

3. Notice when your inner dialogue is critical. Gently pause and breathe. Then say: *I love you YOUR NAME*. This will feel strange at first. You may laugh or hate it. But, this will interrupt the pattern of jumping to self-criticism.

4. Be aware of any **victim thinking** like…

I have to work so hard for very little results.
I feel so frustrated all the time by how many things go wrong.
Why can't something go right?
I'm angry that no one will help me.
I'm angry that I have to work hard for a few results while other people get quick results and are stupid!
I feel like I'm constantly pushing this rock up a hill and I'm tired.
Why is this so hard?
I have to do as others want so they won't be mad at me.
I feel stuck here and I don't know what to do.
I won't be able to fix this.

WISH YOURSELF COMPASSION

I'm ashamed for feeling this way.
I'm not doing enough.
I am not enough.

High-Vibe Thinking™

I have compassion for myself.
I deeply and completely love and accept myself.
As I heal, I grow.
I have compassion for how hard it is to carry this fear.
Even though I've been hurt, I am healing and growing.
I deeply and completely love and accept myself.
I am love. I deserve love.
I am on a healing journey to greater self-compassion.
I have compassion for what I've been through.
Please help me heal my heart, so I can be free.
I am love, I am divine love.
I am giving and receiving only love.
I notice, breathe, and send myself love when I judge myself.
I am here to learn and grow.
I am a work in progress.
I am doing the best I can.
I am working on forgiving myself.
I am on a journey to self-forgiveness.
I deserve self-compassion.
I choose self-honesty over self-criticism.
I treat myself with kindness.

Book Group Prompts

1. What do you have compassion for within yourself? (your fear, anger, shame…)
2. Do you have compassion for yourself to the same degree that you have it for others?
3. What will you do going forward to build more self-compassion?

6. Make the Most of Your Time Here

Our mortality, while scary, is a gift. It reminds us to not waste time.

> "We don't get to stay
> on this earth forever.
> Our time is quite short
> regardless of our endeavor.
> The truth is -
> it's time for my body to die.
> We may not feel ready,
> but we need to say goodbye."

When we live each day appreciating the temporariness of life, our problems and circumstances are viewed as temporary. Because one day, we don't know when, we will be gone.

So, what will you do with your time here?

It's easy to say: *Make the most of life!* But, when we're hurting, it's not so simple. It's nearly impossible.

Having a positive attitude, while pushing down your pain, doesn't work.

A better strategy is what you'll see in the coming chapters…

Allow all emotion, while keeping your thoughts supportive.

This is a process of chipping away at an iceberg.

Bit by bit, we **move old emotional energy out** and we become lighter, less dense.

Moving out *old energy*, loving yourself, and sharing your talents and gifts is making the most of your time here.

MAKE THE MOST OF YOUR TIME HERE

You were sent here for a reason.

You're brave to face all of the hard stuff so that you can fulfill that destiny.

Toolbox

1. Whatever has happened in the past that has hurt you and you're still carrying it, **plan to heal it** so that you will be more and more present and powerful. Principles 7 through 10 will address this more.

2. Be less busy. When you overschedule yourself it can be too much. Create enough time to rest and refuel.

3. Practice being in the moment. When you're in the past or future, notice and think: *Be here now. Thinking. I am here.* Say any mantra that brings you back to the moment.

Don't be discouraged when you find this difficult and it seems like you just can't stay in the moment. You're human and *the pesky ego keeps pulling us out of the moment.* But, you can win over the ego in the end.

4. Practice expressing yourself honestly.

Emotional expression: Express how you feel when it's important to you.

Personal expression: Find a form of personal or creative expression that's enjoyable and feeds the soul. Whether it's painting a wall in your house, fixing an old car, creating a garden, cooking, or writing poetry… *express yourself.*

High-Vibe Thinking™

I am here now.
Be here now.
I'm in the present moment.
I won't waste my time.
I don't waste my beautiful time.
I give myself permission to protect my energy.
I give myself permission to protect my time.
In my free time, I choose who I will spend time with.
I spend time with people who lift me.
I spend time with people who bring out the best in me.
I am in situations that expand me.
I am in situations that help me learn and grow.
I love time.
I respect my time.
I am with others who respect my time.
I attract people who value me.
I attract people and situations that make the most of my time.
In my free time, I have every right to choose what I'll do.
I love spending my time doing what I enjoy.
I am filled with joy at the moment.

I notice what's going on around me.
I am grateful for my life.

Book Group Prompts

1. Does the temporary nature of life influence your choices? Does it motivate you?
2. How could you make better use of your time?
3. Going forward, what specifically will you create more time for?

7. Drop into a Hole

At some point along your soul's path, unfortunately, you'll probably experience heartache.

Giving yourself the space and grace to grieve, honor your life experience, and heal emotionally is extremely important. In the fable, I call this initial place: *the hole*. We visit it when we need to.

During your time in the hole, you don't want to see light. This is a nurturing time of quiet and connection with the *sacred otherness of life*.

THE BUTTERFLY SILHOUETTE

In this place, and maybe long afterward, you fear never being happy again. You may feel guilty. You may feel regret and shame. I felt all of that. All of these emotions are natural and valid.

We feel it to heal it. That's how the body is made. Feeling your emotions slowly releases the fear, guilt, shame, regret, anger, etc. living within you.

Here's what you can do to help the emotion along: When an uncomfortable emotion comes up, **feel the emotion while turning off your thoughts.**

But, here's the tricky part…

You will want to think about why you feel a certain way. You'll want to think about it with every cell in your body.

You want to go over and over why it happened, how it happened, who did you wrong, how you're right, they're wrong, how unfair it is, and so on.

Thinking about it is natural. However, at some point, you must stop feeding the emotion with negative thoughts.

Negative or low-vibration thinking keeps the pain alive.

DROP INTO A HOLE

It's hard to pull away from negative thinking; however, you can slowly train your brain to *not do this*. It takes time. Stick with it as part of your spiritual path and personal growth. The brain can be reshaped over time, but we must stop grabbing onto our negative thinking.

Through this work, you transcend generations of mind conditioning, creating a more harmonious existence for yourself and the world around you.

Toolbox

1. When you have an uncomfortable emotion like anger, regret, fear, envy, guilt, shame, anxiety…

Pause and breathe.

Notice how it feels in the body. For example, your chest feels heavy or tight, your throat feels dry, your stomach is nervous and upset, etc. Just notice. *Feel the energy of the emotion directly. Be patient with yourself. You deserve love and care.*

You're breathing gently while you do this. Notice your energy shift as you breathe.

As you breathe, if it feels good, picture yourself surrounded by bright white healing light. Let it hold and calm you. One breath sequence that works well is to inhale for 4 counts, pause, and then exhale for 8 counts.

Also, here's a useful emotional release method I created called F.A.C.E.

DROP INTO A HOLE

Face the emotion (feel the energy of the emotion).
Accept and allow it.
Choose high-vibe thoughts to support you.
Exhale throughout.

Here's another visual technique I do… Name the emotion you're feeling in the moment, ie: *Fear*. Now, picture the emotion/word in a cloud that you're exhaling. As you exhale, see the air leaving your mouth with the word/emotion inside of it.

Many *emotional release methods* work beautifully. Find one that works best for you. Search online for emotional release methods or Tapping or emotional freedom methods.

2. Beware of your ego in the healing process. The ego is the part of us that judges our emotions and everything else. When I notice myself *judging my emotions*, I tell my judgey ego: *Leave me alone!* I picture my ego as a little gremlin walking away and sitting on a curb on the side of the road. Now, it's no longer bothering and interrupting me. It's separate from me sitting on a curb!

3. When you catch yourself thinking of the past or future, return to the present moment. Thinking about the past or future feeds your fear, guilt, regret, anxiety, and anger.

4. Use high-vibe thoughts after you've allowed yourself to feel the emotion.

IMPORTANT NOTE - If you're feeling too vulnerable to be in a hole by yourself, seek help from a professional bug or go to the hole another time when you're ready.

DROP INTO A HOLE

High-Vibe Thinking™

I am safe. I am secure. I am ok.
Feel this emotion, don't feed it with my thoughts.
Breathe.
Breathe.
I picture myself surrounded by bright white healing light.
I am not ready to surface and it's ok.
I am healing my life so I can be free.
I am being held as I go through this.
I am not alone as I go through this.
I feel a supportive Presence as I feel my emotions.
This healing time is sacred to me.
Please hold me through this.
I deserve a life free of old heavy energy.
I deserve to be free of the past.
I allow myself to feel and heal.
I let myself feel the full range of my emotions.
I can handle this.
I know that part of my purpose is to heal the past.
As I heal, I am a good example to those I love.
As I heal, I have more love to give.
I am ready to surface.

Book Group Prompts

1. How much time do you spend feeling and healing your emotions?
2. Do you carry uncomfortable emotions around a lot? Which emotions are you experiencing most?
3. What will you do to nurture yourself while in the hole? (The hole is the place of emotional healing and personal growth.)

8. Let Your Sadness Run Through You

When Kat is ready, she leaves the hole. But, she's not quite prepared for the light.

She keeps moving forward, one leg then the other.

Continuing to be with her sadness, Kat leaves the hole and enters a puddle underneath a tree. The puddle is **a well of all healing, created by the rain.**

THE BUTTERFLY SILHOUETTE

Think of *the hole* in Principle 7 as a kind of *triage* after something painful happens so that you can catch your breath and soothe your soul.

Meanwhile, **the well** is a safe place to be with your emotions as an ongoing part of personal growth and healing.

We come into this life with a legacy—so to speak. **We're carrying old emotional energy that takes time, patience, and commitment to be free from.**

While you're in the well, your intellect doesn't serve you.

> "Your intellect won't work in here,
> it's useless at these depths.
> Leave your logic on the shore,
> over by those stoney steps.
>
> This is a well of all healing—
> *what doesn't heal will continue to bleed.*
> Let your sadness run right through you,
> though it's very hard indeed."

LET YOUR SADNESS RUN THROUGH YOU

While you're in the well, *let your sadness run through you* (or any emotion you're holding.) I speak to sadness specifically because it's often underneath emotions like anger and fear.

We're sad about who and what we've lost in life, what we didn't get that we needed, and how we've been hurt.

Sadness

There is great power in *letting your sadness run through you.* Let it run through you by feeling the emotion while not holding on to your negative thoughts.

Or, said another way: *Lean into the energy of the emotion without feeding it with your thoughts.*

This place of self-honesty and self-love opens you to the mysteries of life.

During the caterpillar's quest, in this place of sadness, she is visited by the butterfly's soul. She's able to have this illuminating conversation because her brain is worn out.

Her mind no longer blinds her to the mysteries of life.

Somehow, when we allow our experience fully, we open up to our destiny.

We allow our experience fully by being present with what's happening at the moment.

While you're in the well with your hurt, anger, fear, etc., stay afloat because you're designed to heal. Every single human being is designed to heal.

Toolbox

1. To practice sitting in the middle of the emotion, *face the emotion directly within yourself without thinking about it.*

This is the same as Principle 7, we're just practicing more. I'm speaking from personal experience when I say it's not an easy thing to do. *Trust that you're not alone in the well, a*s I discuss in Principle Two, *Ask for Guidance.*

Each time you show up for the emotion, without feeding it with your thoughts, you're releasing old emotional energy that no longer serves you. This is part of evolving your soul.

NOTE: If you feel too vulnerable in the puddle, swim to shore or don't go in. Seek help from a professional bug or go to the puddle another time when you're ready.

High-Vibe Thinking™

I am not alone in this well.
I am safe. I am secure. I am OK.
Feel this emotion. Don't feed it with my thoughts.
Breathe.
I picture myself surrounded by bright white healing light.
I allow myself to be sad without shame.
I am not alone in this place.
I am healing my life, so I can be free.
I need a break from this, so I will take one!
I'm going to go do something else that feels lighter.
I am designed to heal.
I am strong enough.
I am getting the help I need.
I need to talk with someone.
I need help.
I believe in my ability to heal.
Sadness changes as it moves through me.
Sadness can be gentle.
Sadness is part of the human experience.
I am healing my past so I don't bring it into the present.
Even though I'm very sad, I deeply and completely love and accept myself.

Book Group Prompts

1. Does your sadness lighten as you honor it over time? Think of something you were sad about earlier in life… has the sadness decreased over time or is it still strong for you?
2. Which emotions are you having beneath your sadness?
3. What are these emotions telling you that you need?

9. Believe in the Plan for You

Six months after my husband passed away, he visited me in a dream. Except that it wasn't a dream, *it was a dream visitation*.

A dream visitation is when a deceased loved one communicates with us while we're sleeping.

At the beginning of the visit, I asked him, *where have you been?*

THE BUTTERFLY SILHOUETTE

He said…

> "I had important things
> it was time for me to do.
> I came back down here briefly,
> just to talk to you.
>
> I want you to know I'm fine.
> I'm where I need to be.
> I'm watching everything you do,
> there's nothing I won't see."

I wrote it in the fable almost exactly as he said it to me during the visit.

And, when he said he was only visiting, like Kat, I was heartbroken.

> "So you're going back?
> You're not here for good?"
> Kat's heart breaks again.
> She misunderstood.

I was heartbroken to hear that he was going back, he wasn't alive. He was still gone.

Honestly, it took me a long time to accept—*he is still gone.*

BELIEVE IN THE PLAN FOR YOU

Years later, this dream visit has been a source of tremendous comfort. And, **it opened me to a new way of seeing life and death.**

Then, he went on to say that I had more to do with *my life*. I had my destiny to fulfill on this side. He said,

> "Let me tell you a secret,
> that few in the garden know—
> *You have someone you're meant to be,*
> though you don't think it's so."

From his elevated perspective, he knew I had more to do with my life. And interestingly, he knew I would doubt it! He knew it would take me time to believe in myself.

His visit transformed me. He helped me believe in myself and a bigger plan for my life.

You don't need a dream visit from someone you love to begin the process of believing in yourself.

> *You have someone you're meant to be,*
> *though you don't think it's so.*

THE BUTTERFLY SILHOUETTE

He didn't tell me WHAT to do—he only said there was a plan for me. I had to figure out the rest.

Trust there is a plan for you as well.

Toolbox

To build belief in what is possible for you, *do all of the principles in this book and when you're done, repeat.*

These principles are necessary because when we doubt ourselves and live in fear, we make choices based on doubt and fear. This is free will.

Our destiny is there, but it doesn't happen automatically. We do the inner and outer work to make it happen.

If you're doing the work and things still aren't as you'd like, trust that you're learning something you're *meant to learn.*

Everything I've done has taken WAY longer than I thought it should.

Keep noticing and allowing fear and self-doubt, while keeping your thinking high-vibration as described in chapters 7 and 8.

Remain open to what the best use of your life is and trust that the universe is helping you along. Let the plan evolve. It will become clear.

THE BUTTERFLY SILHOUETTE

Here's where we are so far, with slightly different wording:

1. Commit to your destiny.
2. Make quiet time to hear guidance.
3. Notice the quality of your thinking.
4. See yourself on a soul level
5. Have compassion for yourself
6. Make the most of your time
7. Drop into a hole with your grief and heartache
8. Sit in the middle of your sadness

Belief in your destiny takes time, attention, and commitment. While it can be tough at times, enjoy the process of your evolution.

High-Vibe Thinking™

I believe in myself.
I am committed to uncovering my destiny.
I can do this.
I will do this.
I am doing this.
I have a reason for being here.
I am a co-creator of my life.
I am creating my life.
Even if I don't know the plan for my life yet, I will at some point.
I trust that the universe has a plan for me.
I trust that I have everything I need to execute that plan.
I have the talents, gifts, intelligence, resources, and energy to fulfill my destiny.
I am building belief in my soul's plan.
I am doing the work to fulfill my potential.
I am doing the work to fulfill my destiny.

Book Group Prompts

1. What do you believe is the plan for your life?
2. Do you seek guidance from whatever you believe is the *sacred otherness of life* and what does that sound like?
3. Do you feel heard?

10. Pry Yourself Free

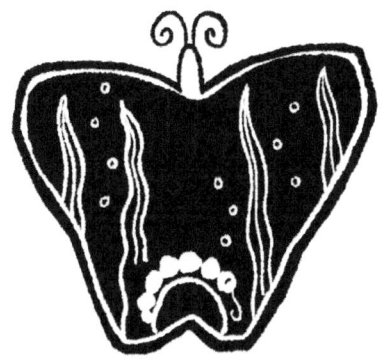

As you heal your heart, you pry yourself free… *from the stoney impingement you cannot quite see.*

We've all been hurt and disappointed by life. When you're hurting, imagine yourself in a *well of all healing created by the rain.*

And, you're not in there alone.

When Kat is stuck beneath the stone and doesn't know what to do, in surrender she utters—*I love you.*

THE BUTTERFLY SILHOUETTE

"I love you,"
Kat hears herself say.
She leans into the stone
and the stone moves its way.

When Kat says *I love you*, she says it to herself, God, the puddle, and the butterfly.

She loves herself enough to respect her emotions and life experiences.

This is how we let go.

We love ourselves while we feel and let go. Feel and let go.

Letting go doesn't mean you go from feeling something at a 10 to a zero. At least it hasn't been for me. Instead, letting go has been a dialing down from 10 to a 1, 2, 3, or 4, depending on the day. It's a breaking up of old emotional energy.

Beastly Bugs

I include this so you won't feel discouraged by the slowness of letting go.

The challenges you've carried for most of your life— think of them as beastly bugs.

For example, feeling not good enough in some way.

Being afraid people will disappoint or hurt you.

Being afraid that life will let you down.

Being afraid you will lose people or things that mean everything to you.

Whatever it is for you…

The beastly bugs may be with you for much of your quest.

Think of them as *gentle reminders* of where you are healing and growing.

THE BUTTERFLY SILHOUETTE

Beastly bugs will tire as you do this soul work and play.

They become quieter and quieter because you keep moving forward. *You're not weak because you still hear them.*

You're strong because you keep moving forward, one leg then the other. You're awesome for doing this crawling work.

Toolbox

1. Name 3 beastly bugs you encounter most often. For example, feeling not enough, shame, heartache, etc.

2. Remind yourself that you are bigger than they are. *Commit to feeling and healing emotions that bother you.* Refer to Principles 7 through 10.

3. Trust that nature heals us. As you feel, intending to let go as you learned in Principles 7 and 8, you dial down the bug's yammering.

High-Vibe Thinking™

I love myself through this.
I respect how I feel.
I accept what's happened in my life.
I will get through this.
I am free in this life.
Each time I let go, I am more free.
I don't have to stay stuck here.
I am stronger than I think.
I am stronger than I know.
The universe is holding me.
I am feeling what's true for me.
All of my feelings are valid.
I do not judge my feelings.
I can handle this.
When I can't do it, I step away and do something comforting.
When I don't feel safe, I ask for help.
It is my destiny to heal my life.
It is my destiny to be emotionally free.
I am designed to feel and heal.
Nature has designed me to heal.
I honor what I'm feeling.
I breathe throughout.
Breathe.

Book Group Prompts

1. What is one of your beastly bugs? If you're not comfortable saying it, that's OK too.
2. What would you say to the beastly bug? Kat yelled at him to leave her alone, ignored him, and ultimately, was indifferent to him. What specifically would you say?

11. Love Yourself

It's part of your destiny to love yourself unconditionally.

Think about the circumstances you were born into: the wounded parent, the loss of someone you love, the uncertainty and fear, etc.

It's challenging—and yet, we judge ourselves for not doing life perfectly and smoothly. We think everyone else is doing it better. But, they aren't.

You are a unique individual with a one-of-a-kind soul.

THE BUTTERFLY SILHOUETTE

You're unique down to the memory in your cells. On top of that, you have your temperament, personality, physical body, emotional challenges, and life lessons.

Your soul's road is not like anyone else's. People who judge you should probably look at their own life, not yours.

Part of growing self-love is doing the inner and outer work of healing.

In the fable, the caterpillar enters a *well of all healing created by the rain*. Inside there she's with her grief, sadness, and anger. After a time she surfaces, but she asks the universe to stay with her…

> She looks to the skies
> with eyes that can see,
> "Keep healing my heart
> so I can be free."

She will continue healing her heart—with new eyes.

Kat sees the world differently because she's operating at a higher level of self-love.

LOVE YOURSELF

Keep healing my heart, so I can be free.

How long does this take?

How long it takes depends on how much heavy emotional energy you're carrying and the strength of your desire to be emotionally free.

Keep in mind that your soul desires self-love and emotional freedom, and you have everything you need to get there.

Toolbox

1. Say to the universe each day: *Keep healing my heart so I can be free.* Or choose wording that resonates with you.

Make it your clear intention to be emotionally free.

2. Ask yourself: *What is my biggest challenge right now?*

Affirm: *I can and will love myself through this.*

Affirm each day: *Even though this is a challenge, I deeply and completely love and accept myself.*

3. Continue feeling emotions directly without feeding them with negative, low-vibe thoughts.

LOVE YOURSELF

High-Vibe Thinking™

I deeply and completely love and accept myself.
Keep healing my heart, so I can be free.
I feel my emotions while not feeding them negative thoughts.
I accept all that has happened.
I'm a work in progress.
Here's what I've learned…
Here's what I'll do differently.
I no longer reject myself.
I give myself the time I need.
I give myself the space I need.
I intend to be emotionally free.
I love myself enough to let myself feel this way.
I am love.
I deserve love.
I am giving and receiving only love.
I am living my highest truth.
I am allowing my greatest healing.
Thank you for keeping me in love's way.

Book Group Prompts

1. Who does Kat say, *I love you* to?
2. Along your self-love journey, what have you learned to love and accept about yourself?

12. Fill Your Silhouette Out

You have a destiny.

Regardless of your spiritual beliefs, religious beliefs, or no beliefs at all—your life is NOT a random occurrence.

You are meant to be the fullest expression of your soul as a human being.

You have specific things you're meant to learn and give.

Near the end of the fable, Kat sees a butterfly silhouette in the distance. She recognizes it as hers, but she's still afraid.

THE BUTTERFLY SILHOUETTE

> "Is it too big,
> this new life I see?
> The largeness of the wings
> terrifies me."

When you recognize your destiny, the thing you *must be and do*—you'll be asked to step inside.

When you've been doing this *crawling work*, even though you're afraid, you're more ready than you think.

The unknown can be scary, and you may stumble and fall, but you'll be OK. It's your destiny to keep moving forward.

When Kat steps inside her silhouette, changes take place.

> Unaware that she knows this,
> Kat forms leaves in a pile
> and creates a chrysalis
> that she sleeps for a while.

> Kat stays there for days
> while her whole body changes,
> every part of her being
> completely rearranges.

FILL YOUR SILHOUETTE OUT

Her destiny shows her what to do next. Nature flows in its natural order.

When Kat awakes, she's moved to tears. The future she didn't believe was possible, has happened.

> When Kat awakes,
> she notices her wings.
> Her eyes fill with tears
> from all that change brings.

Your destiny is meant for you. And while it may take a while, it's yours.

You may doubt it along the way, but keep doing the *12 Principles of Metamorphosis* and your destiny will move closer to you.

You've dared to face your fear, face yourself, and continue moving forward.

You have someone you're meant to be.

THE BUTTERFLY SILHOUETTE

> She unfolded her wings
> in a moment of bliss.
> "I had no idea
> it would be like this."

Toolbox

1. When you begin seeing what you need to give and heal in this life, notice any fear or resistance you may have. Assure yourself… I'm OK. It's natural to be afraid when you see the bigness of your destiny.

2. Watch closely the quality of your thinking as you step through fear and resistance. Use the tools you learned in Principles 7 and 8 to move through your fear.

3. Trust your instincts about what's right for you. **You've done this soul work so you'll see yourself more and more clearly.** You will know what is right for you. Step inside your silhouette and let destiny do
the rest.

High-Vibe Thinking™

I believe in myself.
I trust myself.
I am moving forward, one leg then the other.
I am stepping into my destiny.
Hold me through this exciting time.
I love living this way.
I am filled with joy over expressing what is within me.
I look forward to helping others with a similar path.
I know I was created for this.
I trust that I will know the steps to take.
I allow the path to unfold in front of me.
I had no idea it would be like this and I receive it ALL!
I am receiving all that is good in my life.
I deserve full expression and bliss.
I deeply and completely love and accept myself.

Book Group Prompts

1. Do you sense that you have someone you're meant to be?
2. What are 3 things you're meant to give?
3. What are 3 things you're meant to learn?

12 Principles of Metamorphosis

1. Commit to your destiny
2. Ask for guidance
3. Notice what's beautiful
4. See yourself on a soul level
5. Wish yourself compassion
6. Make the most of your time here
7. Drop into a hole
8. Let your sadness run through you
9. Believe in the plan for you
10. Pry yourself free
11. Love yourself
12. Fill your silhouette out

About the Author

Jeanne Nangle, coach and author, grew up in Southern California within the Jewish faith. She earned both her bachelor's and master's degrees from California universities. In her late 30s, Jeanne felt a deep calling to explore the soul and its role in human life. This journey intensified in her 40s after the passing of her husband, a profound loss that deepened her spiritual practice and commitment to her soul.

Jeanne Nangle is the author of two critically acclaimed inspirational self-help books, she's taught high-vibe thinking™ to doctors and their staff, and she writes a spiritual blog that has helped countless people throughout the world find self-love, authentic self-expression, and follow the soul where it must go.

www.jeannenangle.com